SPARK YOUR CREATIVITY

AN INTERACTIVE GUIDE FOR IGNITING YOUR IMAGINATION

Copyright © 2023 by Niddhish Puuzhakkal

Acknowledgement

It is with deep gratitude and appreciation that I acknowledge the countless individuals who have inspired and influenced the creation of this book, Spark Your Creativity: An Interactive Guide for Igniting Your Imagination. This book is a testament to the transformative power of creativity and personal growth, and its effectiveness is a result of the collective wisdom and experiences of everyone I have had the privilege of working with as a Creativity Cognitive Coach and Personal Life Coach.
From my clients, colleagues, and educators, I have learned valuable lessons about the process of creativity, self-reflection, goal-setting, and taking action to achieve our dreams. To all of you, I offer my heartfelt thanks.

HOW TO USE THIS BOOK

The true value of "Spark Your Creativity: An Interactive Guide for Igniting Your Imagination" lies in the extent to which you incorporate its insights, guidelines, and exercises into your daily life. Merely scanning the chapters will not suffice; you must put into practice what you learn and fully engage with the exercises. Only then will you reap the full rewards of this valuable resource.

Make Concentrated Ritual

Set aside a dedicated time where you feel more receptive. It's better to do these exercises in the morning or evening, or both. You can also apply some of these exercises right before an important assignment, project, or presentation. This does not preclude a casual reading at your leisure and discretion. But do this ritualistically till the time you start seeing results.

Pen it down

As and when you will engage in the exercises, Make sure to jot down any thoughts and ideas that may surface . When a idea pops in your head or a method resonates with you . Spend some time to decipher that thought or idea. Think about it in connection with your life, work, project, and lifestyle. Think about how it could change and improve what you are doing . Think about how you can apply it , visualize yourself doing so and making it pay off for you . Think about a future from now where you have used these techniques and have found success – see your self in that moment, what are you doing in that future? how have you improved your creativity? how much success have you achieved ? What can you hear or feel when your success is at its pinnacle?

Make a note of those visions as well, whether it's an audio recording or a written note. Add the date next to it so that you can track your progress. Add an acronym to some of the thoughts to remind yourself of them and to help you take action in the future. Then start reading again.

Taking action

It is impossible to make any headway or accomplish much of anything until intellectual thought or insight is combined with proper action and follow-through. So once you have grasped a particular idea or process and know how to apply it, take action and put it to work in your daily life. The results may be immediate or may start showing slowly, but if you are determined to use it again and again, you will soon discover that you are creating exceptional creative work because of these processes. You'll also discover that setting bigger goals and being creative come naturally to you. You will also develop winning relationships and enjoy life more.

You can use it on your own or with your Creativity cognitive coach.

INTRODUCTION

INTRODUCTION

In a word, this book is about Creativity.

While it shares certain similarities with other books on creativity, this one is not a quick fix for coming up with ideas or a magic bullet for increasing your output. Whereas, you will still be able to achieve the same thanks to the book's findings. What you'll find is a genuine, straightforward, and process-oriented interactive training programme and techniques here that will help you uncerstand and connect with your mind and methods to Spark your Creativity whenever you like.

 We are all creative. The type of creativity I am referring to in Spark Your Creativity is not just a rare gift possessed by a chosen few. It is a cognitive activity we all possess, a certain detail we apply at every moment of our life – in choosing the clothes we wear to the way we choose to arrange our desk we apply creativity knowingly or unknowingly. it's a thought process which naturally comes up from within, most times unconsciously.

  You are reading this probably in your computer, do you realize that the computer was once a dream in someone's mind. Most of the things around you are in some way a product of human creativity – the pen, the building, the car, the mouse, the coffee mug. What was once an ounce of imagination is now a reality? How did this inception happen? Where is the source of this creativity?

  If you would say it was the education and knowledge of individuals who were able to create – let me ask you how many were there in the same classroom of Steve Jobs or Elon Musk in their school and college. Does everyone with same education and knowledge showcase similar creativity? What's different is what we call Imagination – It brings those dreams to life - It is imagination which makes a possibility and then it is creativity which makes a possibility into a reality.

Imagination and Creativity are instrumental in changing the world from a rock age to now, it is the catalyst to change, always been the only source of hope – Creativity gives a feeling of accomplishment. Yet it also makes people insecure, restless, uncertain and at times anxious.

Creativity can create wonderful things including a lot of problems – it can solve a lot of problems too but Oh boy! can it create a havoc if not managed appropriately.

So What is creativity ?

In many ways, creativity is one of those subjects that people have never been able to accurately answer - it has remained a mystery, and many people regard it as a gift for a select few. While the truth is that creativity is nothing more than a specific way of being and employing a specific set of mental processes. It is explicitly learnable, manageable, and improvable.

Creativity is more than just the ability to come up with novel ideas that can be used to solve problems, create art, or write or entertain. It is also in the simplest of things that we do- including the linguistics we use - how we communicate with each other - sarcasm, even a snorty remark is a result of creativity - a colour or a specific cut that we ask the tailor to make and which we choose to wear - to the personalization we do to our desk involves creativity - the selfie people click involves creativity.

People frequently mix up creativity and artistry. Artistry, is the ability to turn creative ideas into tangible works of art or craft. It involves a level of skill, technique, and craftsmanship to produce something aesthetically pleasing and meaningful. Artistry is often associated with the visual and performing arts, but it can also apply to other fields where skill and craftsmanship are valued, such as cooking or woodworking. but it also involves a significant amount of craft--yes, creativity is part of that --because there is no art without self-expression--but it is still distinct from Creativity. Creativity refers to the ability to come up with new and innovative ideas or solutions. It is the ability to think outside the box and generate something original. Creativity is not limited to the arts; it can be applied to any field or discipline.

From crunching numbers for maximum profits, to a creative sales pitch, to making a speech in a Team meeting , to Composing music, creating a dance routine, coming up with a new recipe, to having a sense of humor, everyone is creative in one way or the other.

Everyone is creative... but not everyone knows how to use or hone that creativity. When I say hone that creativity, I mean an individual's ability to use the information he receives through his 5 senses and how he processes/ distorts/ defines it and then applies it to the response onto a specific task using conscious and subconscious mind.

Certain people naturally use creativity because they discovered these processes and have been using them in a specific way to achieve results. These processes are also known as skills. I'm not saying that having a thought, developing it into an idea, and then turning that idea into something tangible, useful, or applicable is simple. It necessitates unwavering dedication and passion.

Creativity is most applied as a solution to problem – and the type of problems one may face is neither predictable or possible to simplify. Each persons way of addressing a problem will also be different – why because each persons creativity is different – it comes from within the fibre of "individuality".

Each person is creative in their own unique way. It is something we are born with (in some way) and tend to learn on our own, in our own way. And I could bet that most of us are not quite sure how we do what we do when we are being creative. If you ask an artist how he comes up with such beautiful visuals – he probably wouldn't know – he could tell you where he learnt art, how to hold a brush or what he saw.

Most Creative people are like that, largely unaware of what their cognitive process they are using to create. And yet the things we do best are the ones we do unconsciously.

I have asked this question to several creative individuals - Artists, Art Directors, Painters, Music Directors about what was going on in their mind when they did something creative, and the answer was mostly in simpler words"I don't know, i just did it". A very few people knew their own mental systems to answer questions like that probably because of introspection. If you think about it – For a few it is as if their brain is controlled by somebody else. Like a joystick of their decisions is not in their hands. If your brain was really yours, why would it show you pictures of Gulab jamuns (dessert) when you are trying to diet? Why would that voice tell you "Damn it you are going to screw this up again" when you are attempting something you wish to do.

  As part of my process I interviewed several advertising directors on how they would approach directing visuals to a same script – the concept was of metamorphosis of a mobile phone – Each and every directors version of the already written script for metamorphosis was different – While one of them imagined the metamorphosis happening in a jungle as the veils consume the phone and finally giving birth in a different form – Another director saw it transforming robotically like transformer the movie- another person saw it as the mobile phone having feelings another of a phone undergoing labor, I saw it as a metamorphosis of a phoenix turning to ashes and coming back again All of them were fantastic and different.

But when I asked them how they came up with the thought – almost all of them said "I just thought of it like that".

What matters is the mental method we employ to generate original ideas. Like the way we dial phone digits, perhaps. Now You can call a specific number to have Fried Chicken delivered to your office for lunch. You call a different number if you're interested in a therapy. When in a muddle, you might call up your therapist and ask for a Zinger Burger and a six piece hot and crispy. Their bewilderment is easy to picture. And the disappointment you felt when your lunch wasn't delivered when you were starving in the middle of the afternoon. It's also possible to call the Kfc franchise by accident, ask for the lily blossoms, and receive an lily Burger instead. Okay, then you can pat yourself on the back for originality. The names and phone numbers of other highly imaginative persons who you can trust would be very helpful. When you're done with this e-book, I hope you'll have enough ideas for at least four or five pages of a phone book which you can use.

In short, I'll be discussing how we can tell the difference between your mind's activity when you're creative and when you're not. Instead than sitting about and waiting for inspiration to strike, you can instead seize the moment whenever you like and do more of what you want to.

WHERE ARE YOU GOING?

"If you don't know where you are going, you will never reach there."
In order for you to get into the process of igniting and boosting
creativity , it is important to know where you are headed . if you are
headed to Location A – you know you will need to take right where
as if it is Location B- it is a left. Unless we don't have a goal it is
often we will find ourselves floating .

   The Goal for being creative for a particular objective will
immediately link your brain and subconscious mind – aligned
towards achieving that particular goal. The goals serves as a filter,
and a motivation for creativity. Is the purpose to be more creative
to get rich? Or impact the world with your creativity or because
you want to be popular or is it to share your thoughts to the world?
What is the goal of being more creative. Or are you simply bored -
Several people also create when they are upset, or bored or under
pressure. Whereas a few only when they are comfortable or
inspired. This emotion based creativity where the stimuli is the
emotion can get the work done for sure however it can also
become a limitation especially if the stimuli is not a positive one.

Some people often work towards a certain future, and a few other
its an escapism from something they are going through. All of this
comes down to our basic mental systems – beliefs, emotions and
value systems.   It is observed that a certain orientation you
choose to represent a goal will have an tremendous impact on how
effectively you achieve something.   If you look at successful
Creative individuals – why are they successful? Why do some
people find success in the manner they do ? Let's lay out our
criteria for what it means for an artist to be successful.

To be productive as an artist, you need to meet these six criteria.

- The first criteria is Freedom – Freedom from fear – Freedom from guilt and freedom from anger.
- The second criteria is Energy – an energy which keeps them going – we don't get much satisfaction if we don't have energy.
- The Third criteria is The challenge – we need a challenge, excitement, something which pushes your limit are something which gets us up every morning .
- Financial security is the fourth criteria, because we can't have fun if we're constantly worried about money..
- The Fifth criteria is Meaning and Purpose – mans need for purpose is the greatest single drive in human nature.
- Sixth, we need to achieve self-actualization, or the state of mind when we realise our full potential as human beings.

Now this maybe common for an ordinary person – however for a creative person these are extremely important to reach their success. This could might as well be a goal for many of creatives .

Whatever the outcome expected – one of the most powerful strategy for creativity is to develop an internal picture of the outcome you wish to see in your life. The creative process will be to structure the reality to match this internal picture that we create. These needs to be specific to the goals related to your individual self – because the only thing you can control in this world is yourself and guess that is enough. If a parent creating a mental picture of his child to look a different or act differently will not be an effective thing to visualize rather it will create problems.

The goal can be represented more richly by using all senses – and verbal description – emotions and physically stepping into a future . It will also depend on what representational system you are more active in to represent your goal. You will learn more about representation systems in the next chapter.

What a creative individual needs is a compass. Yes the compass which navigators use with the magnetic needle swinging freely and pointing to magnetic north. A sailors best friend, an instrument for showing the right direction or ascertaining the course of his ship at sea. Of course he also uses it to draw circles and taking measurements. The reference here is to the signify that our subconscious mind and conscious mind wants the best for us – it wants us to reach our goals – know the exact direction to use to get to these goals as well. It also know the extent you can push yourself, your intent your limits, your space and time as well your purpose and design. By igniting and activating the internal compass.

Exercise 1: Compass Alignment

- Close your eyes
- Take deep breaths , Relax into a comfortable seating.
- Imagine you are 1 year in the future
- Imagine, Visualize or pretend that you have achieved your goals
- Now record everything you can visualize – what do you see ? What do you hear ? do you feel anything in your skin? Is there any smell ? do you have any taste.
- **Hint :** The only trick here is to let your thoughts, images and feelings flow .
- Think about it for a minute or two- when you are ready open your eyes – now write down all that you saw , heard or felt in that moment where you have achieved your goal

MY NOTES

THE SELF & THE SUBCONSCIOUS MIND

What we did in this exercise is aligning our subconscious mind – to a certain reality – the more we do this exercise the subconscious mind starts believing it's a reality and what it does in return is prepare you with it abundant wisdom it has acquired from the moment you were conceived all that information which never reaches to the conscious mind – it uses all those resources to help you achieve them. While this process may seem simple – it is also very powerful – the 5 senses which we use to perceive the world – is also used to create a future in this exercise . The subconscious mind interprets the reality and reacts basis the information it carriers. When a certain reality such as this is introduced with all sensory information – it has an automatic response of reacting to this reality.

The Hindrance of self –
Something to keep in mind - our brain just like it has been receiving information from our senses – it has also been learning from its interactions – you have been coached, wheedled, bribed, coerced, conned and bullied into seeing reality in a certain way . You conscious mind may believe without an ounce of doubt that this is how the world actually is – and there is only one way see it. All your ideas of how the world is not completely your own. You were born into a ongoing world bought up to accept its rules and definition. So when you do a process which is different – your internal dialogues – what we called Auditory digital – which is where primarily – Most of the comments we have heard from people, parents, teachers – the criticisms we have, the bullies speech , the ridicules, the judgements we have learned and that we may have heard are all stored in.

These information stored will have shaped a certain reality of the world in your mind– if a new process , or any new experience or information surfaces– this reality starts to reject the information. It starts to criticize, generalize or jump onto a quick judgement of what this is, and could be and will be. This is not something we can switch off – however in order to train the subconscious and to completely engage and create an image of the future or to do any psychological process to tap into the inner resources of the sub conscious mind. You will have to make a conscious effort to not to act on these rejecting information you may receive. This map of reality rejection mostly happens in the form of voices in our head – it could also be kinesthetic, or visual.

Hint : Keeping a Journal

- Use a blank spiral book or other notebook
- This is your private growth journal – for your eyes alone. You can share this with others if you like of course. But that should not dictate or influence in anyway how you would keep this journal.
- Personalize the journal – draw a doodle, or write a piece – be creative (geese) ... this journal doesn't have to please or impress anybody but you.
- Every time you do the exercise – write down all that you experience – every minutest detail you can recollect– what you saw, what you heard , the colour, the details, the smell, the taste – who else was there in the visualization, what were you wearing, what was the emotion you had. Was there in a bodily feelings you experienced etc.
- Even while reading this book, feel free to make notes of the thoughts that may come up for you.

THE AWAKENING

 The greater our ability to switch between all these senses makes our experience richer and thus helps to create a richer map of reality and allowing him to direct it for a unique creative outcome. These modalities or styles are, in the simplest terms, different ways in which different people approach the creative process.

Learn to identify your own personal style. If you are not aware of your preferred modality, you may unconsciously design and deliver information in a format with which you are comfortable and as we have heard before – we cant expect a different results by doing the same thing.

So what are the type of commonly use representations of creative Individuals.

Initial - Artistic Visuals

Develops comprehension from visual information and mental imagery. Interpret social cues from a person's posture, facial expressions, gestures, and clothing to infer their intentions.

daydreaming or making up stories in one's head.

Create mental images or patterns to help you better understand the material. Often sitting at a place where they can see everything happening around them (e.g., front of the room).

are typically proficient spellers. Most people are visual learners (e.g., slides, transparencies, handouts, flip charts, posters, or videos). Feel something deep inside when exposed to certain colours and lighting.

Initial – Auditory Originals

Voice characteristics such as rate of speech (words spoken per minute), inflection or pitch (high/low), voice tone, volume (loudness/softness), voice quality (pleasant/unpleasant), and articulation or enunciation of words can be used by these people to decipher the emotional meaning and intent of what is being said (clearly pronouncing words without cutting off endings or slurring). Frequently capable of remembering talks, jokes, and anecdotes and being able to credit them to the appropriate individual.

Primary - Kinesthetic/Tactile Creatives

Participating in an activity or carrying out a task allows one to amass knowledge and improve their level of comprehension, respectively.

The greatest way to learn something is to explain it to yourself, investigate it, play about with it, manipulate it, and put it together or take it apart.

During periods of idleness, there is a possibility that they will get restless or bored.

Meaning and comprehension can be gleaned via touching, doing, and interacting with something.

Choose to interact with people in person whenever possible.

Generally speaking, enjoy being active, yet when working on projects, they frequently leave a mess.

Are psychologically stimulated by the activity of moving about (theirs and others).

Strong gestures and an eager voice quality are frequently utilised as communication devices in interpersonal settings.

Eight Creative Intelligence

Reading, writing, and being able to communicate clearly in a variety of settings are all essential components of linguistic intelligence.

The ability to reason, calculate, think in a logical manner, and process information are all components of logical-mathematical intelligence.

The ability to think in pictures and to envisage a conclusion or a result is one of the hallmarks of spatial intelligence.

The capacity to solve issues or move objects by using one's own body or parts of one's own body is referred to as bodily kinesthetic intelligence (BKI for short).

Someone who possesses musical–rhythmic intelligence can write music on their own, in addition to being able to understand, appreciate, and interpret it.

It is essential to have high levels of interpersonal intelligence in order to comprehend the feelings, characteristics, and capabilities of other people as well as to know how to communicate effectively with them.

Intrapersonal intelligence refers to a person's capacity to create accurate perceptions about themselves and then put that knowledge to use in order to perform effectively throughout their lives.

The capacity to recognise, comprehend, and categorise recurring occurrences in nature is the hallmark of naturalist intelligence.

When you make a map based on a certain sensory representation, it allows you to do things – but it also starts to restrict other ways of perceiving it. In the movie Alladin , for instance – Alladin reaches the cave – where there is no way to enter it . there was no calling bell or a key, no door or a passage. There was just a mountain- he had to figure out that need to switch his perception from what he sees in front of him to Auditory representation system and say " Khul Ja Sim Sim " to get through that door – now that is an effective way to use the sensorial representations for creativity. In another words – it is the similarity which is stopping us from being more effective .

Each of this sensorial representation primary's is designed to perceive varied qualities of the experience. Such as color, brightness, texture, shape, tone, rhythm, volume, hot, soft, sily, pressure etc. These showcase how developed the primary sensorial representation is for the individual.

The first instance that facilitates creativity is a genetic set up of an individual for a given sensorial. It makes sense that a person whose sensory system is more sensitive to color and light will have an upper hand in becoming a visual artist like a painter, or who are born with sharp auditory senses who understand pitches, tones, and acute sounds perfectly may do exceptionally well in music. And helping them being better at their respective fields, they naturally will be inclined and will be deeply interested in sounds and colors, it is only natural for them to learn more about them, and grow in a position to create or innovate in the field of music or art much easily than the other.

On the other hand, having a sensory advantage is not necessarily required in every situation. Lot of artists have been impaired, yet they have become geniuses in a specific field or domain for example: When Beethoven wrote some of his most iconic works, he did it despite having significant hearing loss. This is largely because just the heightened sensorial acuity is not enough – the mindset and the cognitive computations, passion and commitment plays a huge role in what they do with those gifts they posses.

Having said that a special sensory advantage may be responsible for getting a focus towards a particular field or domain which happens much early in life, which is certainly an important ingredient of creativity. Lot of creative individuals showcase interest in a particular domain this is also a place where parenting and support and will to achieve comes into play. Certain individual digress from their core interest basis the experiences and life structure and may never develop these sensory advantages. Where as a few other may sharpen these skills to make something out of their lives.

A huge aspect of it is also pertaining to an individuals curiosity, wonder, and interest in specific things – a questioning mind is always the beginning of creativity- what things are like and in how they work. For this reason children are naturally creative because they are extremely curious and open to experience – their attention is fluid and they process their surrounding environment with great novelty. Each and every person that is creative possesses an abundance of these characteristics.

Exercise to Amplify Sensorial Acuity:

Building Visual Acuity (A Powerful exercise for the visual artists, designers)
1 . Sit comfortably in a location or position of your preference.
2. Gaze around the room and memorize as many of the objects in your room as possible.
3. Put your mobile audio recording on.
4. Now close your eyes.
5. Try and remember all details in the room. (Don't cheat)
6. Now try and remember each of them in depth- what colour is it, what is the texture, what is the shape of the items in your room , does it reflect light, is this opaque or transparent. – describe each of them to record.
7. Open your eyes – look around – did you get all of them right? Now listen to the tape the way you described it . Is there a difference? Could you have added more detailing ? Did you completely miss any item which was right there in front of you. Were you inaccurate about anything.
8. Now close your eyes again – think of all the elements once again – now add the missing details – now amplify its colours in your mind – add the textures to it – now change the shape of it.
9. Now describe how you see it and record.
10. Open your eyes – compare from the first to second tape.

MY NOTES

MY NOTES

You will learn something valuable about your observation of the same detail – also you will realize the second time your cognition makes creative choice – not stopping at adding enough to fill in the gaps it goes beyond to change things to more richer arrangements.

Now imagine doing this on a visual project – and test it.

Building Auditory Acuity (A Powerful exercise for musicians, performers, sound designers also for individuals to improve listening skills)

1. Sit down in a comfortable position
2. Put your mobile audio recording on.
3. Close your eyes
4. Focus on the noises and voices around you . Try and remember all of them in great detail. The pitch, the volume, the feeling it generates. Describe it in great detail on to the recording.
5. Open your eyes – listen to the audio recording (Use a decent headset or ear phone) – increase the volume of the recording – did you miss any sound or voice .
6. Now leave the phone aside close your eyes again – focus on the noises and sound once again – now mentally increase the volume of the sound, focus on the texture, the pitch, the bass . now describe it and record it.
7. Now open your eyes – compare both of the recordings . Now listen to the noises and voices around you .

You will notice your auditory senses have become very alert and active.

MY NOTES

MY NOTES

Building Kinesthetic (Physical/Emotional) Acuity Acuity (A Powerful exercise for actors, performers, also helps individuals build better relationship and to be perceptive of other individuals and emotions)

1. Sit down in a comfortable position
2. Put your mobile audio recording on.
3. Close your eyes
4. Now focus on the bodily sensations – is it hot, is it sweaty, how does your skin feel on back of your neck , on the tip of your toe. Record this in great detail.
5. Open your eyes – listen to the audio recording .
6. Now close your eyes again – focus on body sensations again – now mentally increase your sensitivity until you feel whatever you felt earlier has increased. now describe it and record it.
7. Now open your eyes – compare both of the recordings .
8. Now just focus on your breath –

You will feel your receptivity of your skin has increased.

MY NOTES

MY NOTES

Note : Now remember for certain individuals – with an inactive or less active sensorial acuity will take time to show dramatic difference in the exercise – however you will notice the more times you do this exercise your sensorial perceptions are improving tremendously .

Also certain mental blocks and mindset as discussed in the chapter will engage your mind with auditory digital or auditory resistances which will try and distract or stop you from a new experience or focussed experience. Simply because its new and are not used to it . You will have to play a traffic cop – just diverting the emerging thoughts and resistance to pass by and focus on the task at hand.

THE IRREVERANCE
METHOD

To enhance your creativity, and to think outside the box, first and foremost thing we need to do is get back to basics of life. Just like how senses the most basic thing can be such useful tools in cognition for creative mastery.

The second most basic thing is that our major learning of the world and its structured happened when we are children. We learned adult behaviours, we learned to make sense of the world, we learned the do's and donts and the sets of rules.

Every act of creativity is already contains a certain skill that a person has to attain. Once an individual acquires a skill , he learns techniques , and then creates a set of rules to do them. As a popular belief – every rule can be broken – you can then bend or break the rule in a informed manner and that becomes artistry or creativity.

When we were Children, during the ages we learn language, we use something called as representation of the words. If we observe a child we can see they like experiment with the words and how they represent them is usually unique and poetic. They create this sentence things, they sing songs with the new words, alter different words to make different noises . We also notice children get animated about everything they see and perceive. We see them acting like an ambulance running around the house using the sound of the siren, we can see them behaving like a cartoon character or mimic an adult without any inhibhition . This is also a way they make sense of things . There is a focused and intense participation to every new information they receive and process.

Children use all opportunity for expression, they also use play. Infants are seen playing from an early age on in their development.

Infants as young as 7 months old can be seen actively taking part in the game of Peekaboo, which needs the complex sort of playing described as a "game" that adheres to rule structure.
Undoubtedly, play is the earliest form of human expression, predating even language.
There are currently three classes into which expression can be placed.

Another important aspect of childrens development that's observed is the their natural irreverence – they will keep pushing boundaries to know how far they can go. They understand very soon that someones status, or being a grown up or a stranger does not hinder them from doing what they are focussed on doing . This irreverence can be seen in their language expression where they combine words to create new meanings which may not be part of the rule book. The way they would use their emotion expression will also most times unpredictable and irreverent . The picturing expression also showcases irreverence and rebellion.
Reverence is good for neither the revered nor the revering. The revered gets no honest feedback, only adoration. The revering learns to not challenge the status quo and to value honorifics above ability. Everyone is deluded about the revered's practical worth.

Irreverence is healthy skepticism. It promotes constructive discourse. It opens the possibility of proposing fundamental change. It lets people think outside the box.
Individuals who embrace irreverence without fear of making mistakes are more likely to produce significant creative outputs. Rebellion also confirms a certain uniqueness . It is an appropriate and normal part of a child's develop- ment to rebel. Around two years of age, it is normal for the child to say 'no' to a host of demands from its caregivers. This negativism allows the child the oppor- tunity to test the waters of autonomy.

Adolescence, in addition, is notorious as a period of rebellion, and quite likely is a crucial epoch for the adolescent to establish an identity separate from the identities of others.
Creativity commonly involves two struggles: the struggle to have one's ideas accepted and the psychological struggle for finding order. Creativity is itself an inner struggle to rebel against chaos, apathy, and death. All rebellion, ultimately, is a rebellion of the self.

We all have daily instances where deviance not only con- firms our identities but also is an antidote for alienation in the face of oppression and impersonal conformity.

It seems self-evident that there are times when conformity is a good and useful thing. For example, it is important for automobile drivers to conform to the rules of driving, other- wise there would be total chaos on our roads; individualized patterns of driving would be very dangerous, and it would be impossible to predict what any given driver would do. On the other hand, the conformity of blindly sending people to their deaths by execution during Hitler's regime was a bad type of conformity.

Probably the single most prevailing symptom of ineffective rebellion is the individual's unwillingness to understand or pay the price of the rebellion. Effective rebels are fully aware of the consequences of their decisions and actions. Benedict Arnold presents an example of ineffective rebellion.
It is evident that irreverence and rebellion are one of the essential tools for creativity. Sir John Hegarty – the prominent advertising personality quoted in his book –

Creativity, according to this definition, entails the frantic assembly of seemingly unrelated ideas and emotions in order to produce a new perspective. For this reason, we can only describe it as magical. It's true that you should follow a procedure if your goal is mediocrity.

The truth is that the world is rife with predictability; we know exactly what we'll see on TV whenever we turn it on, we can guess how any given story will conclude, and so on.
Reason being that society as a whole has conditioned original thought to follow a set of predetermined rules.
It's something that would naturally occur in the arts sector.
The process is an attempt to bring order to an otherwise chaotic situation. The creative process entails generating disorder intentionally. Both are extremely extreme examples of their respective categories.

Irreverence, if it comes from a place of love, an understanding for the absurdity of the human struggle to accept and make sense of its own mortality, may be wonderful. In the hands of talented artists, irreverence may be a highly original and refreshing viewpoint. We can put the veracity of apparently holy institutions or ideologies to the test in a humorous way through irreverent inventiveness.
We are able to bring out the inherent flaws in false idols without resorting to violent destruction because we are not simply creating with irreverence but also with art, craft, and originality as we do so. George Carlin, for instance, took on one of the most revered theological structures in history when he opined that the Ten Commandments was too much. It was a "padded list," he remarked.

While doing so, we would benefit from developing a dose of healthy irreverence to spark the creative process and allow us to poke fun at ourselves when we get too serious, too petty, or too focused on the small stuff in our lives.

The reason the most successful people are irreverent is because they learn from other people's lessons and think to themselves they can do better. They do not hold the falsified perception that the 'respected' have the best answer, instead they question them always. Staying irreverent means to stop thinking in the mindset of others and starting thinking in your own.

 So how do we develop irreverence for creativity and not be irreverent for the sake of irreverence. However it is important to understand irreverence in general requires courage and conviction to stand by what you produce or create. if you are that person this method will do wonders for you.

Exercise : The irreverence Method

This exercise require some sort of a project to see the fantastic result it can offer . however for demonstration purpose – we will

Step 1 : Take up a project you have in hand -
- Flip a positive statement into a negative one in an ongoing endeavour.
- Use negative connotations to explain what something is not.
- Learn to give accomplishment to someone who has none.
- Shift a viewpoint to a new location or orientation.
- Flip-flop the arrangements
- Transform a loss into a win, or a win into a loss.

Step 2: Turn the affirmation into a negativity
For a brand brief on art, for instance, you would brainstorm all the possible ways in which art could be portrayed negatively.
Some of the ideas you have will surprise you in a good way.

Step 3: Going Against the Norm
Apple Computer beat IBM in computer sales, and Japan leads the world in producing compact, fuel-efficient automobiles.

Step 4: The "What-If Compass"
Draw up a list of contrasting solutions that could be tried.
Simply fill in each polar opposite to the question "What if I...." and see what happens.

A small sample:-
You can either elongate it or compress it.
Cool it down or heat it up
Edit it to make it more or less about you...

Step 5: The fifth action is to shift your viewpoint. Shift in one's physical stance, To maintain control, get up and move about, or try something new.

Step 6: Reversed Outcomes

Perhaps you should consider lowering prices if you want to boost sales. What would it require on your part?

Step 7: Reverse a previous successful outcome.

Do not let a bad outcome derail you from considering the bright side. If I lost all of the files from this computer, what good would come out of it? Maybe then I'd be able to devote more time to my loved ones! The answer may surprise you!

You will realize that you were able to create something absolutely creative. Now imagine applying this consciously- would this produce some new ideas? Imagine writing about a character – would he be more interesting ? Would this work to better acting skills ?

Because every single person we know is always trying to do the right thing, it has become too usual and boring . often when someone does or says the wrong thing – its refreshing and interesting. Break a rule of artistic expression – see how what that creates – Surprise people. Do the polar opposite of what you would ordinarily do, such as taking an unexpected stance or making a ludicrous analogy. People will take notice if it comes as a surprise to them.

MY NOTES

MY NOTES

THE UNKNOWING METHOD

The creative process we are going to discuss in this chapter is all about "not Knowing" . Most of the time we look at something, or hear something or a subject comes up – the first response that naturally comes to us " I know this" which immediately creates a mental map – which is based on your experience and recollection. However as discussed in previous chapters – the mental map by itself is a interpretation or a alternate reality which we have created basis the sensorial information received – and our mental states and emotions. " I Know This " Immediately set up this map built on one of these representational systems and this has the huge potential to limit you.

When a new information is presented and it poses a question in your mind "if you know what this is?" And if your answer is "Yes, I know this." Immediately you've put one of those existing maps up in your mind and you've matched it with something on the outside. You have met your criteria for "I know" and you often stop from any form of new creation or building new sensorial information .

If an individual could approach something with a " I don't know what this is" that creates a child like curiosity, a fresh perspective that allows your mind to make new maps . The reason children are far more creative than adults is because they are an empty canvas – there is no existing maps that they link to every single thing they are presented with . The most powerful thing that we could develop is the ability to remake maps as and when we like to. One more reason to immediately bring up a map is because of success that we may have found in the past experience. The "success" sometimes can be a biggest hindrance to creativity – because we have found success at a certain time – we empower that map of reality so much that we often do not even think beyond it.

When something works – we keep doing more and more of it – if tooth paste in colour work – we keep making newer colours . if an apps model works – we build industry around similar apps.
More than often I have seen organizations stressing to create new models based on previously successful models – they will spend millions to ensure to follow the same process to build the new one. And more than often what they produce don't seem to be in anyway significantly different. But that's obvious because if the map of reality and the approach is the same.
All I am saying is that "success" can be a limitation unless you are willing keep an open mind. It is not going to be easy at all to be successful in a particular thing – to pull out of that and to keep aside the success to stay more receptive to new maps . Because your mind will keep repeating this to you – that you know it . However if you manage to do it – you will start seeing Novelty, newer richer maps gets created and what you will create will look fresh and exciting.

Take Barry Marshall, an Australian physician. In 1984, Marshall went to a major meeting of ulcer specialists in Brussels, Belgium to present his data indicating that bacteria were the likely cause of ulcers. The audience of ulcer specialists thought his talk was ridiculous and laughed it off.
Marshall returned a year later with even more convincing evidence after drinking a vial of germs and giving himself an ulcer, but was met with a chorus of boos from the group. It took ten years for the American Medical Association to embrace Marshall's research and announce that bacteria, not stomach acids, stress, or spicy foods, are the predominant cause of ulcers, contrary to what previous studies had suggested.

The Nobel Prize in Medicine was shared by Marshall and his research collaborator, Dr. Robin Warren, in 2005.
This raises the obvious question of why, for over 20 years, hundreds of thousands of ulcer sufferers were subjected to unneeded, expensive, and frequently useless treatment.
The reason for this is because many people, including highly trained medical specialists, dealt with the issue by saying, "I know."

You cant fill a cup that's already full could be another way of looking at it . However what we are talking is a bit deeper than intelligence – we are not talking about knowledge or skills here . Learning and intelligence is linear and se-quential – we acquiring "know"ledge about a subject, how to operate within the parameters and its rules . Once we know about the subject – is when cognition begins – this is where creativity begins. By knowing the rules and its paradigms – helps us bend them or to ignore or alter or completely change them.

More familiarity means less mental stimulation.
The most stimulating concepts are those that challenge us to generate new connections in order to make sense of the world around us when we are thrown off our usual mental track.
"Whack on the Side of the Head" is how Roger van Oech describes it, whereas Edward deBono's "Provocative Operation" (or "PO") is his original term for the phenomenon.
Schedule some breaks into your day. Try a new route to work, a new radio station, a new magazine, a new book, a new recipe, a new TV show, a new movie, or even just a different shift at work or a different day of the week.

A provocative thought can serve as a springboard to additional possibilities A common practise in the East (such as haiku poetry and Zen koans) that can feel awkward to Western minds is abutting concepts next to each other so that their friction develops new thought-paths.

What we are talking about cognitive openness to any thing presented to you.

For example – if you working on a brand for years, and know well – momentary forget all about what brands been good at and have been successful in . approach the brand as if you are hearing about it the first time – What does the brand stand for ? what archetype is the brand – is it 1 or more ? What would such a brand should do ? Whether it's a brief from from a client or a shot to be taken or a piece to write . Step into the "Unknowing" and then begin.

Exercise : The "Unknowing Method"

This exercise require some sort of a project to see the fantastic result it can offer . however for demonstration purpose – we will use it to something simpler.

Sit down in a comfortable position
Look at a person who maybe in front of you or passing by.

Think how much do you know this person – you will realize there is an immediate set of details about him that has kicked in – something about the way he is, where he comes from, what type of a personality or character he possess.

Now make 5 bullet points about this.
Now go to a new page . Now Consciously forget everything about the person. and start wondering about who he could be – what would his personality be like, how would he speak ? Imagine you have never met him/her before and you are wondering. Now if you could talk to this person and ask questions about him.
Now make a few bullet points about this conversation.

Now compare both the points . you will realize there are several new things that you have know about this person – your premade judgements and asessments have stopped you from knowing this person more deeply and profoundly.
Now apply this same technique on an object and see.

MY NOTES

MY NOTES

MY NOTES

Imagine using this technique in a client brief, or when trying to solve a problem. Most times what we know and what success we got could be hindering our creativity as it stops us from exploration and wondering.

Now I do not mean we forget the basics for example – I am not asking you to forget his name or what he does – and asking them something that you know or everyone knows would sound bizzare. What I am trying to drive is the idea of wiping the slate clean and approaching a project or a person or an object to give us a instrument to think and create beyond what we know.

THE MEMORY METHOD

The Subconscious is where all of your memories are stored. Though it stores information outside your awareness better than any other part of your mind, your Unconscious Mind also controls your feelings and your body's mechanical processes. Before thinking about this line, you probably weren't aware of your feet touching the floor or your back touching the chair. Constantly, sensations are being sent to your physical body, but you are usually oblivious to them. Your Unconscious Mind also regulates your heart rate, blood pressure, digestive processes, and lymphatic system, among other things, so that you can feel well physically and emotionally. That causes your eyes to blink automatically. Knowing that your Unconscious Mind controls everything like a well-oiled machine is a wonderful thought.

We will primarily focus on the idea that your Unconscious Mind may have a two-way conversation with every single cell in your body. The entire scope of the Mind/Body relationship is now being appreciated by scientists. Scientific studies have shown that your thoughts, emotions, and actions have a direct impact on every single cell in your body, 24/7.

Neurons are the cells in the nervous system responsible for transmitting electrical impulses that carry information and memory throughout the body. A gap, or synapse, exists between any two neurons. Something must be responsible for transporting nerve impulses across the spaces between nerve cells. Chemical messengers called neuro-transmitters carry impulses along the axons that connect nerve cells.

Neuro-transmitters were found to link every neuron in the body, creating complex "electrical circuits." Quantum physics and quantum biology have revealed that neuro-transmitters permeate every human cell. To fully understand the Mind/Body relationship, this new information is essential.

The Unconscious Mind not only coordinates our feelings, actions, and bodily processes, but it also sends signals to and influences the trillions of cells that make up our bodies, producing either health or dis-ease in accordance with our unconscious assumptions. Our body is always listening in on our thoughts. The mental and emotional states, as well as the ideas and information processed by your mind, are all registered by your body. Your immune system is continuously influenced by the activity of your Unconscious Mind via the conductivity of the neuro-transmitters that surround all cells.

Isn't it true that the beginning of our power to materialise a number of great things is to access all that memories stored in our body? To what extent is reality a construct? In what ways does one remember? A imagination...what is that?

When contemplating the mysteries of the Unconscious Mind, we inevitably run into the age-old conundrum, "What is real?" Since nothing is'real' at the Unconscious level, this is a problem only with the Conscious Mind.

Maybe we may also ponder, "Is the Unconscious Mind real?" The Unconscious Mind cannot be real because of the meaning of the word "real," which denotes "having substance." The obvious follow-up query is whether or not this implies that our recollections are not actual.The answer is yes and no – our mind constantly alter, distorts, exaggerate and modify information basis our experiences and emotions. The same memory after a certain period of time may seem a little different to you, or it may seem different to you in a different state of mind as well. Now the essence of the memory maybe the same – but if youobserve closely you will notice the exaggerations, the colours may seem different, the settings may have changed. This is also the reason why trauma seems so vivid to many , a certain incident is constantly processed and made richer in the mind strengthening thos unfortunate traumatic visuals in the mind . and every time that memory kicks in the person starts trembling with strong emotions associated to it.

The link between the physical and mental realms is also the portal through which we cross into the fantastical. To understand the 'unreality' of the Mind, we must first accept that the Real is the 'physical. As you come to understand that All is Mind, you will be in a position to facilitate people's openness to change.

That all we perceive around us is an illusion, or "Maya," is a central teaching of our vedic teachings, according to our Gurus. As soon as this remark makes sense to you, you will have understood the "unreality" of everything we know to be true. That's some serious heightened consciousness right there. For decades, Zen Buddhists ponder paradoxical koans before they finally grasp the idea that all reality is predicated on the mind's interpretation and creation.

Learning about "the unreality of reality" might help you deal with it and use it to create more vivid memories stored in your body, since you'll have a better appreciation for how much information your body stores compared to your brain. It can be altered almost instantly. One of the most fascinating cases on record is that of a diabetic woman who has several personalities; her narrative highlights the topic of what is real and allows you to quickly ignite your mind and body at any time and experience those memories which are ingrained within you.

The woman's dangerously high blood sugar was revealed during a test of her diabetic personality. Her blood sugar was normal when an attendant took a sample as soon as she shifted to her non-diabetic self, before her body had a chance to filter the blood through the liver and kidneys. It's important to ask, "Where does this diabetes come from? The question is, what is truth?"

Exercise : The "Memory Method"

This exercise requires some sort of a project to see the fantastic result it can offer . however for demonstration purpose – we will use it to something simpler.
Sit down in a comfortable position
Look at a object or a person who maybe in front of you or passing by.
Now close your eyes
Feel relaxation all over your body
Starting from your toes to the tip of head , the muscles in arms and your face all relaxed.
Now imagine a time in your past where you have played with a similar object. Now physically extend your arm and imagine, or visualize or pretend that you are holding the object.
Now look at the object in your hand – is it heavy ? how does it feel ? is it cold or hot? What colour is it?
Now Why should this object exist? is this object really necessary?
Where is the best place for this should this object to be kept?
When do you think this object should be used?
Who should use it? A male , female ? older, younger ?
What all can be done with this object?
How should it be done?is there a best way to use this object?
Can this object be Adapted?, Modified?, Substituted?,
Magnified/Maximised? Minimised/Eliminated? Rearranged? Reversed?
Combined? then how would it look like and what can it do?
After careful observation .
Now open your eyes
Now make a few bullet points from your observation.

MY NOTES

MY NOTES

You will notice there are several new ideas and perspectives which has formed about the object, what you have done is two things –
1 you have used an aspect of memory and had intentionally changed it with questioning it.
2nd because you altered your memory suddently the object in front of you has become fresh and new for the brain to comprehend hence was giving more attention to it. Also the effective question has put a flow your creativity.

THE DREAMER METHOD

When you wake up after a dream, do you ever find yourself asking, "What the heck was that all about?" Dreams are not only capable of being strange and perplexing, but are also extremely potent instruments for the purposes of self-discovery and creative endeavors. In this chapter, we are going to investigate the many modes of dreaming that are present in our brains, and we will also introduce you to The Dreamer Method, which is a strategy for utilising the power of your dreams to accomplish the things you want in life.

When we are dreaming, our brains are functioning in a manner that is distinct from when we are awake. Dreams that involve Rapid Eye Movement (REM) and dreams that do not involve REM are the two primary categories of dreams. Dreams that occur during the REM period of sleep are often the sort of dreams that are the most vivid and easy to remember after waking up. The non-REM stages of sleep are characterised by dreams that are often less vivid than those experienced during the REM periods. Even though REM sleep brings about the most vivid and interesting dreams, non-REM sleep also has the potential to shed light on the events and feelings we go through on a daily basis. Our brain waves are more rapid and less regular during the stage of sleep known as rapid eye movement (REM), which is the period of sleep during which we often have dreams. Because of this, even if our bodies are absolutely still, our brains are operating at a much higher level of activity.
 The brain is going through a breathtaking electrical symphony, which occurs hundreds of times during the course of each night on the surface of your brain, can also assist in explaining your loss of external consciousness.

It begins deep within the thalamus, which is located underneath the surface of the brain. It is important to keep in mind that when we are in the process of falling asleep, the thalamus, which is located in the centre of the brain and acts as the "sensory gate," prevents the transfer of perceptual signals (such as sound, sight, touch, etc.) to the cortex, which is located at the very top of the brain. Not only do we lose our feeling of consciousness when we do this, which explains why we do not dream in deep NREM sleep and why we do not keep explicit track of time, but it also permits the brain to "relax" into its default mode of functioning.

This state, which we refer to as deep slow-wave sleep, is the default one. It is a condition of brain activity that is active and purposeful while still being extremely synchronized. Although it is close to a state of nighttime cerebral meditation, I feel the need to point out that the brainwave activity of this condition is considerably different from that of waking meditative states. In this shamanistic condition of deep NREM sleep, you may find a genuine treasure trove of mental and physical advantages for your brain and body, respectively; we will thoroughly explore the riches that can be found in this state of dreaming. However, one advantage of the brain, the storage of memories, is worthy of more discussion at this point in our narrative since it provides an excellent illustration of what those deep and sluggish brainwaves are capable of. Have you ever gone on a lengthy road trip in your car and observed that the FM radio stations you've been listening to begin to lose signal strength at some point throughout the journey? AM radio stations, on the other hand, continue to exist. It's possible that you've drove to a remote spot and tried to discover a new FM radio station, but you were unsuccessful. However, if you switch to the AM frequency, you will find that there are still multiple broadcasting channels accessible.

The radio waves themselves, namely the two differing speeds that are used for FM and AM transmissions, are the key to understanding this mystery. When compared to AM radio waves, FM radio waves have quicker frequencies and oscillate up and down a significantly greater number of times per second. FM radio waves have the ability to transmit higher and richer loads of information, which results in improved sound quality. This is one of the advantages of these waves. However, there is a significant drawback, which is that FM waves lose their power very rapidly, much like a muscular sprinter who is only able to cover short distances. AM broadcasts use a radio wave that is substantially slower (longer), similar to how an athlete trains to run a long distance. AM radio waves are unable to match the muscular and dynamic quality of FM radio waves; yet, because AM radio waves travel at a more pedestrian rate, they are able to traverse greater distances with less loss of signal. Therefore, longer-range broadcasts are feasible with the slower waves of AM radio, which enable far-reaching communication between extremely geographically separate places.

When your brain transitions from the high-frequency activity that occurs during wakefulness to the lower-frequency, more measured pattern that occurs during deep NREM sleep, the exact same benefit to long-range communication becomes possible. The consistent, slow, and synchronous waves that sweep across the brain during deep sleep open up communication possibilities between distant regions of the brain, allowing them to cooperatively send and receive their various stores of accumulated experience. This occurs because the brain is in a state of "deep sleep." When seen in this light, each individual slow wave of NREM sleep may be compared to a courier that is able to transport packets of information between various anatomical brain areas.

One of the advantages of these brainwaves that pass during deep sleep is a mechanism known as file transfer. Every night, during deep sleep, long-range brainwaves transport memory packets, also known as recent events, from a temporary storage site that is prone to damage to a long-term storage location that is more stable and, as a result, safer. This process is known as "memory consolidation. Because of this, we consider waking brainwave activity to be that which is primarily concerned with the reception of the external sensory world, whereas the state of deep NREM slow-wave sleep donates a state of inward reflection—one that encourages the transfer of information and the distillation of memories. If reception predominates during waking and reflection predominates during NREM sleep, what, then, takes place during REM sleep, also known as the dreaming state? The brain activity that occurs during REM sleep is a nearly exact reproduction of that observed during attentive, awake wakefulness, which is represented by the topline in the image. Recent studies using MRI scanning have shown, in point of fact, that certain regions of the brain are up to thirty percent more active during rapid eye movement (REM) sleep than they are while we are awake.

The knowledge and feelings that we experienced throughout the day are being processed and incorporated into our long-term memories by our brain at this time. Have you ever pondered how it is that dreams may feel so real even though they can be so bizarre? It has been discovered that the mode of operation of our brain during dreams is very unlike to that of when we are awake. When we sleep, our brain activity moves from the left hemisphere, which is responsible for logic and analysis, to the right hemisphere, which is responsible for creativity and intuition.

This paves the way for a deluge of images, symbols, and feelings to rise to the surface. In fact, dreams may be quite realistic, to the point that it frequently feels as though the events within them are really taking place. The reason for this is that the thalamus, which is the region of our brain that interprets sensory information, remains functional even while we are sleeping. It pulls in data from our immediate environment as well as our memories, and then it generates a virtual world inside our heads. The ideas and emotions that are buried deep within us might also have an effect on our dreams.

They can operate as a form of therapist, assisting us in processing and working through feelings that we might not be aware of while we are awake. In this manner, they can help us process and work through our problems. There are several distinct categories of dreams that humans are susceptible to having. Some dreams are little more than jumbled up recollections and feelings, while others are quite realistic and detailed. Lucid dreams are an especially intriguing sort of dream in which the dreamer is aware that they are dreaming and even has some degree of influence over the dream itself. These dreams have the potential to be quite empowering and to assist us in overcoming our various concerns and phobias. The Dreamer Method is a strategy that involves working with one's dreams in order to accomplish one's goals. The first thing you should do is get into the habit of maintaining a dream notebook.

Keep a notepad and a pen next to your bed, and as soon as you wake up, jot down any dreams that you can recall from the night before. After a certain amount of time has passed, you will become aware of recurring themes in your dreams, and you may even begin to experience lucid dreams.
After you've made it a practise to write down your dreams, you may start to use them to get insight into your subconscious using the information they provide. Keep an eye out for recurring images and ideas in your dreams, since they might shed light on your feelings and the things you believe in.

If you frequently have dreams in which you are falling, for instance, you may be experiencing feelings of insecurity or loss of control in your waking life.

Metaphors, or the use of figurative language to describe something in terms of another, are commonly found in dreams. They are powerful tools for unlocking creativity because they allow us to see familiar objects and concepts in a new light, making us think outside the box.

When we dream, our brains often use metaphors to represent things that are difficult to describe or abstract concepts. For example, we might dream of being lost in a maze, which could be a metaphor for feeling lost in our lives. Or we might dream of a butterfly, which could be a metaphor for transformation and growth.

By analysing the metaphors in our dreams, we can gain new insights into our subconscious thoughts and feelings. We can also use these metaphors as a creative tool in our waking lives. For example, if we're struggling with a problem at work, we might try to find a metaphor that represents the issue, such as a tangled web, and then think of ways to untangle it.

The use of metaphors can help us approach problems from a different perspective and break out of habitual ways of thinking. By using metaphors as a tool for creativity, we can access our subconscious and let our imaginations run wild to come up with new ways to solve even the hardest problems or a creative idea to work on.

You may begin to solve these problems and go over them if you pay attention to the recurring themes in your dreams and work with them. Putting your objectives into perspective via the lens of your aspirations is the last stage in "The Dreamer Method." Spend some time each night, prior to going to bed, mentally achieving the things you have set out to do. Visualize every aspect of your accomplishment and experience the feelings that come along with it. After that, as soon as you come to, be sure to write down any dreams you had that were connected to your objectives. These dreams can give you clues about how you might reach your goals, and they might even give you new ideas and ways to reach them.

Exercise: Dreamer Method

Sit down in a comfortable position
 it's important to suspend judgment and to allow yourself to think creatively. This means that you don't need to worry about practicality, feasibility, or even whether or not your ideas are realistic. The goal is simply to generate as many ideas as possible and to explore new possibilities.
Now close your eyes
Feel relaxation all over your body
Starting from your toes to the tip of head , the muscles in arms and your face all relaxed.

Now imagine - What if money were no object? What will you be doing?

After careful observation .
Now open your eyes
Now make a few bullet points from your observation.

Now imagine - What if I had all the resources I needed? What will you do the project in hand ?

After careful observation .
Now open your eyes
Now make a few bullet points from your observation.

Now imagine - What if I had unlimited time to work on this project?

After careful observation .
Now open your eyes
Now make a few bullet points from your observation.

MY NOTES

MY NOTES

While this may seem simple - they are yet very powerful. These types of questions can help to unlock your creativity and to generate new ideas that you might not have thought of otherwise. The key is to let your mind wander and to explore new possibilities without worrying about how you will make them happen.

You will notice there are several new ideas and perspectives which has come up, some may not be relevant to the current project in hand or the idea you are seeking, However you could refocus the thought actually imagine yourself without the boundaries - you may find your results you seek. Because you altered your creative cells to think without the previous limitations which was creating the mental block for - for the brain now it has become fresh and new for the brain to comprehend hence was giving more attention to it. Also the effective question has put a flow to your creativity.

THE CRITIC

Criticism is a strong instrument that may either make or ruin your creativity. There is criticism that is constructive, and there is criticism that is harmful. It is important to distinguish between constructive and destructive criticism because the former can help you better your work while the latter can have a detrimental impact on your confidence and creativity.

The Critic Method is an approach to handling criticism in a constructive manner and utilising it as a source of inspiration for one's own creative endeavours. One of the most common criticisms that can arise during the Critic Method is negative self-criticism. It is easy to fall into a cycle of negative self-talk when examining ideas and creations. In order to combat this, it is important to remember that creativity is a process, and every idea is valuable in its own way. Instead of immediately dismissing an idea as "bad," take the time to explore why it may not be working and how it can be improved. This will help to shift the focus from self-criticism to constructive criticism, which can lead to even more creative breakthroughs. Embracing your inner critic, gaining an understanding of its motivations, and employing it as a tool for self-improvement are all components of the technique

Acquiring an Understanding of One's Inner Critic
A person's inner critic is a voice that exists inside their head and can either be useful or destructive to them. It is the voice that pushes you to excellence by telling you that your work is not good enough or that you are not creative enough. Having an powerful inner critic can be beneficial in that it can assist discover areas for growth, it also has the potential to cause self-doubt and restrict creative expression.

Applying the Walt Disney Critic Model can be one strategy for dealing with your own inner critic. When analysing your work, the Walt Disney Critic Model recommends considering it from three distinct angles: the dreamer's perspective, the realist's perspective, and the critic's perspective. The idealist sees the big picture and is creative in their idea generation, the pessimist analyses those ideas and recognises potential obstacles, and the critic offers commentary and improvement recommendations. Walt Disney, the famous animator and creator of Mickey Mouse, developed his own version of the Critic Method which is known as the Disney Method. Disney used this method to develop his ideas for animated films and theme parks. During the Dreamer stage, Disney would let his imagination run wild and generate as many ideas as possible. The Realist stage involved examining the feasibility of each idea and determining how it could be executed. Finally, during the Critic stage, Disney would evaluate each idea and identify any flaws or potential issues.

You will be able to analyse your work in a more impartial manner and respond to criticism in a positive manner if you adopt these three distinct views. For example, if you have an idea for a new project, start by brainstorming like the dreamer. Then, examine the practicality of the idea like the realist. Last but not least, pinpoint areas where you can improve, just like the reviewer.

Employing Constructive Criticism to Improve Something

It is important to remember to keep an open mind and be responsive to criticism whenever it is offered. Try to look at the criticism as a chance for personal development and advancement, regardless of how severe it may be. Instead of getting defensive, it's better to take a step back and assess the input in an objective manner. Determine the areas in which you could make improvements, and utilise the criticism as incentive to do better in those areas.

It is essential to bear in mind that not all criticism is deserving of serious consideration. There is a possibility that some individuals will provide you with input that is neither useful nor productive. In circumstances like these, it is OK to treat the comments with scepticism and proceed with life.

Asking for specific feedback is an additional helpful strategy that can be used for making productive use of criticism. Instead of asking for feedback on your performance in general, you should ask the person to point out one or two specific areas in which you could improve. This can make it easier for you to concentrate on making specific adjustments and avoid you from feeling overwhelmed.

Incorporating the Critical Thinking Process into Your Creative Workflow To begin incorporating the Critic Method into your creative process, first make some room in your schedule to objectively analyse the work you've produced. This may mean adopting the three views of the Walt Disney Critic Model, or it could involve creating specific goals and reviewing your progress towards those goals. Another possibility is that this would involve setting goals for yourself and analysing your work towards those goals.

It is also beneficial to surround yourself with individuals who are prepared to give you honest critique while at the same time being supportive. Seek for mentors, friends, or coworkers who can provide you with critical feedback and assist you identify areas in which you may improve and talk you through the process.

Last but not least, always keep in mind that constructive criticism is not an assault on your originality or your value as a human being. You may stimulate your creativity and make your work better over time by welcoming your "inner critic" and making positive use of constructive feedback.

Exercise: Inner Critic Integration

To integrate your inner critic into your creative process, try this self-hypnosis exercise:

1. Sit down in a comfortable position and take a few deep breaths.As you inhale, imagine yourself filling up with positive energy and creativity, and as you exhale, imagine any negative or critical thoughts leaving your body.
2. Close your eyes and visualize yourself entering a peaceful and serene space, such as a garden or a beach. Imagine that this space represents your creative mind, and that everything in it is positive, supportive, and nurturing.
3. Next, imagine that your inner critic appears in this space. See it clearly and vividly in your mind's eye, and allow yourself to observe it without judgment.
4. Ask your inner critic what its motives are and what it is trying to achieve.what it wants to say to you. Listen to its message without becoming defensive or reactive. Acknowledge what it has to say and thank it for its input.
5. Next, ask your inner critic if it has any constructive feedback for you. Ask it to provide specific, actionable suggestions that you can use to improve your work.
6. Listen to your inner critic's response and take note of any suggestions it offers. Then, imagine yourself integrating this feedback into your work, using it to fuel your creativity and make your projects even better.
7. Ask your inner critic to provide specific feedback on one area of your work that you can improve.
8. Listen to its response and imagine that these feedbacks are getting incorporated, visualize a future where the product or idea with those inputs have been created, what do you see, hear, feel? what benefits or success have you achieved?
9. Finally, imagine yourself leaving the peaceful and serene space, feeling renewed, refreshed, and inspired. Take a few deep breaths and open your eyes, feeling energized and ready to create.

MY NOTES

MY NOTES

MY NOTES

THE INTEGRATION

Within the field of Neuro-Linguistic Programming (NLP), we make use of an effective technology known as parts integration. It is a technique that assists in bringing together all of the many components of our mind and body so that they can function in concordance towards the accomplishment of our goals. Every one of us is made up of numerous components, each of which is accountable for a particular facet of our being, including our feelings, thoughts, beliefs, values, and behaviours. These components are not always compatible with one another, which can result in a lack of clarity, paralysis by analysis, and restricting beliefs.

The premise of this technique is that every part of our mind and body is doing everything to keep our best interest in mind, but sometimes, it can give the opposite effect.

Our mind is made up of various parts, which may conflict with one another. For instance, a person might have a part that craves unhealthy food, while another part is committed to maintaining a healthy diet. When these parts conflict, they can lead to stress, indecision, and a lack of progress towards goals.

In the field of Neuro-Linguistic Programming (NLP), the idea of parts integration proposes that every component of our mind and body is, in reality, acting in a way that is most beneficial to us, despite the fact that this may not always be apparent to us. Integration of our different parts enables us to access the resources and capabilities of all of those parts, which in turn can lead to more creative and effective thinking, decision-making, and problem-solving.

NLP parts integration is a process that involves identifying and acknowledging the various components of our mind and body, gaining an understanding of those components' functions and purposes, and then integrating those components together in a manner that facilitates the achievement of our goals. This procedure assists in resolving internal conflicts, lessening the impact of unpleasant emotions, and boosting our capacity to accomplish our objectives.

Find a spot that is relaxing, comfortable, and free from distractions so that you may start the process of integrating the NLP parts there. To bring your mind and body back into a state of peace, simply take some slow, deep breaths and concentrate on how you are breathing. Now, picture yourself having a conversation with all of the many components that make up your identity, acknowledging their presence and gaining an understanding of the unique roles that each of those parts plays.

To get started, pretend that you are having a conversation with the aspect of yourself that longs to be more creative. Ask this portion what it needs in order to have a more creative feeling, and pay close attention to what it has to say in answer. The next step is to have a conversation with the aspect of yourself that is preventing you from moving forward and ask that aspect what it requires to feel secure and at ease. Pay attention to the response of this component as well.

Now, picture how all of the disparate components that make up your being are coming together, like pieces of a puzzle, to form a whole that is unified and complete.

Imagine that they are fusing together, each component bringing its own set of skills and resources to the table, and the whole thing coming together in a way that enables you to achieve the results you are looking for.

While you are going through this process of NLP parts integration, it is important to keep in mind that every part of your mind and body is there to serve you in some manner, even though it may appear that the opposite is the case at times. You may unleash your full potential and become a more creative, confident, and successful person by bringing together all of the diverse aspects of yourself.

In parts integration, we ask all the parts within ourselves to integrate together to become the most creative person. By integrating these parts, we can resolve inner conflicts and achieve greater harmony and clarity in our thinking.

Here is an exercise to help you integrate your parts:

1. Find a comfortable and quiet place to sit down and relax. Take a few deep breaths and focus on your breathing.
2. Visualize yourself standing in front of a door. This door leads to a room where all of your internal parts are waiting for you.
3. As you open the door, you enter the room, and all of your parts are present. Each part is represented by an image or symbol.
4. Take a few moments to greet each part and acknowledge its presence. Thank each part for its contribution to your life.
5. Start talking to each part, one by one, asking it to integrate with the other parts to become one unified creative force.
6. Visualize each part merging together, creating a new image or symbol that represents the integrated parts.
7. Continue this process until all of your parts have integrated together.
8. Finally, visualize yourself standing in front of a mirror, looking at the new image or symbol that represents your integrated parts. Take a few deep breaths and focus on the feeling of wholeness and harmony within yourself.

MY NOTES

MY NOTES

SUCCESS AND CREATIVITY

Just tune everyone out.

 Ignoring everybody can be a useful strategy for finding success as a creative. When you have a novel idea or a unique perspective, seeking validation from conventional sources can be counterproductive. In fact, the more unconventional your ideas are, the less likely you are to receive support from those around you.

Many successful creatives have found that they had to tune everyone out in order to pursue their vision. They often faced resistance and skepticism from friends, family, and even professional associates who were uncomfortable with change and disruption. The fear of the unknown and the desire to maintain the status quo can make it difficult for people to embrace new and innovative ideas.

Moreover, relying on others for validation can be tricky because people often have their own agendas and biases that can cloud their judgment. Close friends and colleagues may not be able to understand your vision and may not have the same level of passion and dedication as you do. This can lead to frustration and disappointment when they don't provide the feedback or support you need.

By ignoring everybody, you can focus on your own intuition and creativity. You can explore your ideas without the constraints of other people's opinions or expectations. This can be liberating and empowering, as you can experiment and take risks without worrying about whether your ideas will be accepted or rejected.

Of course, it's important to seek feedback and collaboration at some point in the creative process. However, it's crucial to first establish a strong sense of self and confidence in your vision before seeking outside validation. This will help you stay true to your creative vision and maintain the passion and commitment necessary to bring it to life.

In conclusion, ignoring everybody can be a useful strategy for finding success as a creative. It allows you to tap into your own intuition and creativity, without the constraints of others' opinions and expectations. While seeking feedback and collaboration is important at some point, it's crucial to first establish a strong sense of self and confidence in your vision. With persistence and dedication, you can bring your unique perspective and ideas to the world and make a significant impact.

The idea need not be ambitious. Just that the entire world needs to resonate to it and change because of it.
They are altogether two different things. Our time is often spent being awed by those we have never met. a person with a significant media presence due to their association with a large firm, product, film, or bestseller. Whatever. More time is wasted on our futile attempts to match their rate of progress. We're all trying to get our own things off the ground, whether they're businesses, goods, movies, books, or what have you. I share the blame with the rest of you.
Creating, whether big or small, is an important aspect of personal growth and fulfillment. It is a way to express oneself, share one's ideas, and contribute to the world in a meaningful way. The act of creating, in itself, can bring a sense of purpose and accomplishment that can boost one's self-esteem and confidence. It's important to keep creating, even if the idea is not ambitious or world-changing. The act of creating something, no matter how small, can lead to bigger and better ideas. Each creation is a step forward, a learning experience that helps us grow and develop our skills. It allows us to experiment with different techniques, approaches, and ideas, which can lead to breakthroughs and innovations.

Moreover, creating helps to keep us in a state of flow, where we are fully engaged in the present moment, and our minds are free from distractions and worries. It is a form of meditation that can reduce stress, anxiety, and depression, and promote mental wellbeing. Every creative act, no matter how small, has the potential to make a difference. It may inspire others, spark new ideas, or lead to a new discovery. It may even change the world, in some small way. The important thing is to keep creating, to keep putting our ideas out there, and to keep learning and growing.
So, don't worry about whether your idea is big or small, ambitious or modest. Just keep creating, keep learning, and keep growing. The act of creation is its own reward, and the impact it can have on the world is immeasurable.

Spend some serious time on it.

Putting in effort that yields results is a time-consuming endeavour. Time, effort, and stamina are the main differentiating factors between those who succeed and those who fail. The fact that I've been writing, and making films , and working on Creativity Coaching for so long gives the artwork an edge. Spending serious time in creating is an essential aspect of producing high-quality work. Whether you are an artist, writer, musician, or any other type of creative professional, dedicating sufficient time to your craft can make a significant difference in the outcome of your work.

Creating is a time-consuming process, and it requires focus, discipline, and perseverance to produce something that is truly remarkable. It is easy to get distracted by the multitude of things that compete for our attention, such as social media, emails, and other responsibilities. However, to create something truly special, it is essential to dedicate some serious time to it.

When you spend serious time in creating, you allow yourself to get into a state of flow. This is the mental state where you are fully immersed in the task at hand, and you experience a deep sense of focus and enjoyment. Flow can be elusive, and it requires a considerable amount of time to achieve. The longer you spend on a creative task, the more likely you are to experience this state, which can lead to more innovative ideas and a better final product.

In addition, spending serious time in creating allows you to experiment, make mistakes, and iterate. The more time you dedicate to your work, the more opportunities you have to try new techniques, explore different ideas, and refine your approach. This can lead to breakthroughs and new insights that you might not have achieved with a shorter time frame.

Furthermore, spending serious time in creating helps you build a strong work ethic. It requires discipline, commitment, and a willingness to put in the effort required to achieve your goals. By dedicating yourself to your craft, you develop a habit of working hard and persevering through challenges. These qualities are essential not only in the creative field but in all areas of life.

In conclusion, spending serious time in creating is essential for producing high-quality work, experiencing flow, experimenting, and developing a strong work ethic. Whether you are working on a big project or a small one, dedicating sufficient time to your craft is key to creating something that truly resonates with your audience and the world.

Remember you are born Creative
Creativity is a fundamental aspect of being human, and it is true that everyone is born creative. From the moment we are born, we begin to explore the world around us and use our imagination to make sense of it. As children, we are naturally curious and have an innate ability to think creatively, using our imagination to create new and exciting things.
However, as we grow older and become more socialized, many of us begin to lose touch with our creative abilities. We start to prioritize conformity, following the rules, and meeting the expectations of others over exploring our own unique creative expression. This process can be exacerbated by formal education, where there is often a focus on learning specific subjects and following established procedures, rather than on fostering creativity and original thinking.
Despite this, it is important to remember that creativity is not something that is limited to a select few individuals. Everyone has the capacity to be creative, and the more we allow ourselves to explore and express our creativity, the more we can develop and enhance it.
In fact, many people who believe that they are not creative simply have not had the opportunity to explore their creativity fully. They may have internalized negative beliefs about their own abilities or have not been exposed to creative activities that resonate with their interests and strengths. The good news is that creativity is not a fixed trait, and with effort and practice, it is possible to cultivate and improve one's creative abilities. This can involve setting aside dedicated time for creative activities, experimenting with different forms of expression, and taking risks to explore new ideas and approaches. Ultimately, by embracing and nurturing our creative abilities, we can tap into a fundamental aspect of our humanity, and enhance our ability to find new solutions, innovate, and express ourselves in unique and meaningful ways.

Attempt not to draw attention to yourself by standing out; instead, avoid crowd entirely.

The idea of standing out from the crowd is often seen as an important aspect of success in today's society. However, there is another approach that is worth considering: avoiding crowds altogether. This approach may seem counterintuitive, but it can actually be a powerful way to achieve success and fulfillment in life.

The problem with trying to stand out from the crowd is that it often leads to a focus on external validation. People who are constantly seeking approval from others may find that they are never satisfied with their achievements. They may also become caught up in an endless cycle of comparison, constantly measuring themselves against others and feeling like they fall short.

Avoiding crowds, on the other hand, can allow you to focus on your own unique strengths and interests. Instead of trying to fit in with a particular group or culture, you can chart your own course and pursue your own passions. This may mean taking risks, exploring new areas of knowledge, or following unconventional paths.

One of the benefits of avoiding crowds is that it can help you to develop a sense of authenticity. By following your own interests and passions, you can develop a sense of purpose and direction that is truly your own. This can lead to a sense of fulfillment and satisfaction that is hard to find when you are constantly seeking validation from others.

Another benefit of avoiding crowds is that it can allow you to become a leader in your own right. When you are not beholden to the norms and expectations of a particular group or culture, you are free to develop your own ideas and vision. This can lead to innovation and creativity that is truly groundbreaking.

Of course, it is not always easy to avoid crowds. We are social creatures, and we naturally gravitate towards others who share our interests and values. However, by being intentional about the communities we engage with, we can make sure that we are not sacrificing our own unique identities in the process.

In conclusion, avoiding crowds can be a powerful way to achieve success and fulfillment in life. By focusing on our own unique strengths and interests, we can develop a sense of authenticity and purpose that is hard to find when we are constantly seeking external validation. While it may not be easy, the rewards of pursuing our own paths can be truly transformative.

You can't be hurt by suffering if you accept it.

As a creative person, it is inevitable that you will face these challenges and setbacks. These challenges can come in many forms, such as criticism, rejection, or self-doubt. While these experiences can be painful, they can also be an opportunity for growth and learning. One way to approach these difficulties is by accepting them and not allowing them to cause undue suffering. These people not getting "it" days, and people not seeing your worth is something every creative individual goes through.

Acceptance is a powerful tool for managing difficult experiences. When you accept a situation, you acknowledge it for what it is, without judging it as good or bad. This can help you to see things more clearly and approach them with a sense of calm and detachment. By accepting your suffering, you can avoid getting caught up in negative thoughts and emotions, which can make the experience even more painful.

Comparing yourself to someone else can lead to feelings of unworthiness and inadequacy. It can also lead to resentment and envy, which can be damaging to both the person being compared and the person being compared to. It is important to remember that you are your own person and that you have your own unique voice as a creative person.

That tiny voice inside your head is telling you to get creative. There's a big difference. Your tiny voice doesn't care about book deals or movie deals. Make something, I say. Make something really special. Produce something so mind-blowing that it will astound anyone who sees it. Making something to fit an unrealistic expectation of a market will lead to failure. If you make something special, powerful, honest, and true, you will succeed. The inner monologue didn't make an appearance since it was preoccupied with whether or not you had enough money or hung out with enough celebrities. Your inner being necessitated that tiny voice, so it returned.

It's important that you say or do something, that a certain light be turned on, or that some other action be taken. Now. Therefore, pay attention to the inner voice, or else a significant part of you will perish along with it.

Acceptance is a powerful tool for managing difficult experiences. When you accept a situation, you acknowledge it for what it is, without judging it as good or bad. This can help you to see things more clearly and approach them with a sense of calm and detachment. By accepting your suffering, you can avoid getting caught up in negative thoughts and emotions, which can make the experience even more painful.

It's important to note that acceptance does not mean giving up. Acceptance is about acknowledging the reality of a situation and finding a way to move forward. When you accept your suffering, you can use it as a source of motivation to keep creating and improving. You can learn from your experiences, identify areas for growth, and use your creativity to overcome challenges.

In fact, some of the greatest works of art have been born out of suffering. Creatives throughout history have used their pain as inspiration for their work, creating masterpieces that have stood the test of time. By accepting your suffering and using it as a source of inspiration, you can create something truly beautiful and meaningful.

In conclusion, accepting your suffering can be a powerful tool for a creative person. It allows you to approach difficult experiences with clarity and detachment, which can help you to learn and grow. By using your suffering as inspiration, you can create something beautiful and meaningful that will resonate with others. So embrace your pain, accept it, and use it as a source of motivation to keep creating.

Focus on Passion than Merit

Focusing on passion over anything else can be one of the most rewarding decisions you make in life. Passion is the driving force that can push you to achieve great things and overcome challenges that may come your way. While merit and skill can be bought or developed over time, passion is something that comes from within, and it is not something for sale.

When you focus on your passion, you open yourself up to a world of possibilities. You are no longer limited by what others expect of you or what society deems to be important. Instead, you are free to pursue what truly matters to you, even if it means taking the road less traveled.

However, pursuing your passion requires hard work, dedication, and a willingness to take risks. It may not always be easy, and there may be times when you face setbacks or failures. But if you remain committed and keep pushing forward, you will eventually achieve your goals.

It's also important to believe in yourself and your abilities. Don't let anyone tell you what you can or cannot do. Instead, challenge yourself and take risks to achieve your dreams. Surround yourself with people who support and encourage you, and don't be afraid to seek guidance from mentors and experts in your field.
In conclusion, focusing on your passion can lead to a fulfilling and rewarding life. It may not always be easy, but it is worth it in the end. Remember that success comes from within, and with hard work, dedication, and a willingness to take risks, you can achieve anything you set your mind to.

Finding and Using your Voice
Finding success can be difficult, especially when you are a creative soul. Finding and using your authentic voice is crucial for success in any field. It means finding your own unique way of expressing yourself and standing out from the crowd.

Here are some tips on how to find and use your authentic voice:
- Embrace your uniqueness: You are a unique individual, and you have your own set of skills, experiences, and perspectives. Embrace your uniqueness and use it to your advantage. Don't try to be someone else; instead, focus on developing your own strengths and talents.
- Know yourself: To find your authentic voice, you need to know yourself. Take the time to reflect on your values, beliefs, and interests. Think about what motivates you and what you are passionate about. This self-awareness will help you develop a clear sense of who you are and what you stand for.
- Be honest: Authenticity requires honesty. Be honest with yourself and with others about your thoughts, feelings, and opinions. Don't be afraid to speak up when something doesn't feel right, and don't be afraid to share your ideas and perspectives.
- Practice: Finding your authentic voice takes practice. Experiment with different ways of expressing yourself, and don't be afraid to make mistakes. The more you practice, the more you will develop your own unique style.

Be consistent: Once you have found your authentic voice, use it consistently. Whether you are writing, speaking, or interacting with others, be true to yourself and your unique style. Consistency is key to building your brand and your reputation.
In conclusion, finding and using your authentic voice is critical for success. It requires embracing your uniqueness, knowing yourself, being honest, practicing, and being consistent. By staying true to yourself, you can stand out from the crowd and achieve success on your own terms.

The most important thing you can do is to sing in your own voice.

Do It for Yourself and From the Heart

When it comes to creative pursuits, whether it's writing, painting, or music, it's easy to get caught up in the opinions and expectations of others. You may start to create work that you think will please others or be commercially successful, rather than doing it for yourself and from the heart.

However, creating from the heart is essential to producing work that is truly meaningful and authentic. When you create something from the depths of your soul, it shows in the final product. Your passion, your unique perspective, and your individual voice all come through.

Creating for yourself also has the benefit of allowing you to explore and experiment without constraints. You are free to take risks, try new things, and push the boundaries of what you thought was possible. This process of exploration and discovery can lead to new insights and ideas that you might not have stumbled upon if you were solely focused on pleasing others.

It's important to remember that not everyone will love or appreciate your work, and that's okay. It's impossible to please everyone, and trying to do so will only lead to frustration and disappointment. By creating from the heart, you will attract an audience that resonates with your message and style, and that's what ultimately matters.

In summary, doing it for yourself and from the heart is crucial for producing work that is authentic, meaningful, and true to your voice as a creative. It's a process that requires courage, vulnerability, and a willingness to take risks, but it's worth it in the end when you see your vision come to life.

Caring When Nobody Else Does

As a creative individual, it is common to encounter situations where nobody else seems to care about your creativity or your work. This can be incredibly disheartening and can make it easy to lose motivation and interest in what you do. However, it is important to remember that your creativity is valuable, regardless of whether or not others recognize it.

One of the most important things you can do to care about your creativity is to continue to work on your craft and create, even if nobody seems to be paying attention. When you create something you are proud of, it is important to celebrate it, even if you are the only one celebrating. Recognize the effort, skill, and creativity that went into your work and take pride in what you have accomplished. It is also important to surround yourself with supportive people who understand and appreciate your creativity.

Seek out other creatives who share your passion, and build a community of people who value and encourage your work. This can help you stay motivated and provide a sense of validation, even when others may not understand or appreciate your creativity. Finally, it is important to remember that your creativity is an important part of who you are, and that it deserves to be cared for and nurtured. Take time to prioritize your creativity, even when life gets busy. This can mean setting aside specific time for creative work, or simply finding ways to incorporate creativity into your daily routine. By caring for your creativity, you are investing in yourself and your own well-being, which is something that nobody else can do for you.

Remember to Have Fun

When we're focused on achieving success, it can be easy to forget about the importance of having fun. But the truth is, if you're not having fun, it's much harder to be truly successful. When you're having fun, you're more likely to be in a positive state of mind, and you're more likely to be motivated to keep going, even when things get tough.
One of the keys to having fun is to remember why you started doing whatever it is you're doing in the first place. If you're a creative, you likely started because you enjoy the process of creating something. Whether it's writing, painting, or making music, there's something about the act of creating that brings you joy. When you focus on that joy, rather than on the end result or on what other people might think of your work, you're more likely to have fun.
Another way to have fun is to experiment and try new things. If you're always doing the same thing, it can get boring, and you're less likely to enjoy the process. But if you try new techniques or approaches, you may discover something that sparks your interest and reignites your passion for what you do.

Finally, it's important to remember that success is not just about achieving a particular goal, but about enjoying the journey along the way. If you're only focused on the end result, you may miss out on the small victories and moments of joy that come with the process. By focusing on having fun, you can find success in each step of the journey, rather than just at the end.

Congratulations on reaching the end of this book! I hope that you have found the inspiration and motivation to continue pursuing your creative endeavors. Remember that success is not just about achieving your goals, but also about enjoying the journey and finding fulfillment in your passions. I wish you all the best on your creative journey and hope that you continue to have fun, take risks, and stay true to your authentic voice.

Good luck in all your future creative endeavors!

DRAW A FUTURE SELF OF YOURSELF -
WHERE YOU HAVE ACHEIVED YOUR CREATIVE
GOAL.

MY NOTES

"SUCCESS IS NOT A DESTINATION, IT'S A JOURNEY - AND THE BEAUTY OF THE JOURNEY LIES IN THE MOMENTS OF PASSION, PERSEVERANCE, AND PURPOSE THAT YOU EXPERIENCE ALONG THE WAY."

ABOUT THE AUTHOR

Let me be candid with you for a moment; my name is Niddhish Puuzhakkal.

I've always had lofty goals, ambitious dreams, and the desire to create something incredible with my life; I was fascinated by how the mind worked, and I deeply cared about people.
I come from a humble upbringing, having been born into a middle-class family in a rural part of Kerala, India. My father always encouraged me to pursue a career in engineering, despite my early enthusiasm for the arts and literature. We certainly can't hold that against him, as we didn't grow up in a creative atmosphere and didn't know any people who majored in the arts, fine arts, or filmmaking in college or who have achieved success while learning these subjects.

Consequently, I was tormented because I was different—my abstract art and poems were seen as a joke by many; I didn't associate well with the popular crowd, and my family was always tense—without any understanding of how or why I had become a lost soul. Even though I did well academically, they sure made me feel stupid.

 But when I began taking steps towards my true calling, I was confronted with the next round of life's schoolyard tests: financial difficulties, bewilderment, and rejection. Only by working hard and constantly expanding my knowledge could I afford to pursue my interest. That's what I did, and I'm still learning new things today.

Working hard paid off, and I was able to establish my name in the advertising and film industry while still completing my master's degree in psychology. I am also a Master Practitioner in Neuro-Linguistic Programming, Cognitive Behaviour Therapy, and Hypnotherapy.

I realized our minds and emotions are fascinating when you know how to handle them. When we float through life, we feel we have no purpose or vision, no community, and no contribution to make in life. During this incredible journey of my life, when I began seeking rigorous learning and inspiration on how to create a better life for myself, everything began to change for the better. And I realized this is not the journey of an individual; every single person in this life is going through similar challenges if they are not blessed with the required guidance. I have spent years learning about cognitive modalities and psychology because I realized the answer to the life challenges and creativity is psychology.

Since then, it's been a powerful journey for me. For more than 15 years, I've been a part of the creative sector's workforce. I am a writer, director, and producer. I have written and directed a Bollywood feature film and written and directed over 150 commercials. I mentor aspiring youngsters who want to bloom into their full potential via my experience, skills, and talents in the creativity field. My coaching is not limited to creative professionals; I mentor anyone who wants to excel in the field of creativity because I believe we are all born with it.

As a filmmaker, I am working on my next feature film, which is due to go into production in 2023. I'm a firm believer that living your dream, the mental state you possess, the journey you experience, and the lives you impact are more important than what you do or what you have accumulated. I realized that anything is possible with the right guidance and commitment to any dream or vision, as well as 100% passion to pursue it.

My goal in life is to have a "Positive Impact" on one million people. I I
hope to accomplish this through the films I direct, the scripts I write,
and the lessons I share about following one's passion and tapping
into one's inner resources and subconscious mind to manifest one's
ideal life and leave a positive mark on the world.

I do this through one-on-one sessions, group sessions, training,
podcasts, films, books, online courses, performances, hands-on
workshops, and one-on-one interactions.

If you want to pick my brain, tell me about your experiences, or you
want me to pick yours. Don't hesitate to get in touch.

www.creativitycoach.niddhish.com